Beyoncé

By Sarah Dann

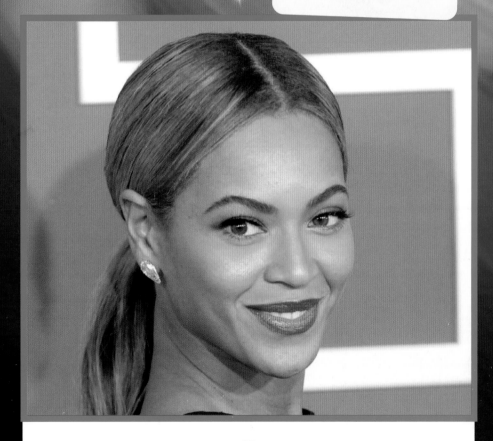

Crabtree Publishing Company

www.crabtreebooks.com

Crabtree Publishing Company

www.crabtreebooks.com

Author: Sarah Dann
Publishing plan research and development:
  Reagan Miller
Photo research: Crystal Sikkens
Editors: Molly Aloian, Kathy Middleton,
  Crystal Sikkens
Proofreader and Indexer: Wendy Scavuzzo
Designer: Ken Wright
**Production coordinator and prepress
  technician:** Ken Wright
Print coordinator: Margaret Amy Salter

Photographs:
Associated Press: cover, pages 19, 25, 27
©Dream Works/Courtesy Everett
  Collection: page 17
Getty Images: Gregg DeGuire: page 6;
  WireImage: page 13; Mark Mainz:
  page 14
Henry McGee/Globe Photos, Inc.: page 21
Keystone Press: zumapress.com: pages 5,
  20, 23, 24; wenn.com: pages 8, 22; Kathy
  Hutchins: page 10; Big Pictures UK: page
  15; Fame Pictures: page 16; EPN/Zuma:
  page 18; EMPICS Entertainment: page 26;
  Mavrixphoto.com: page 28
Photofest: Fox Broadcasting Company:
  page 11; New Line Cinema: page 12
Shutterstock: DFree: page 1; s_bukley:
  pages 4, 7; Featureflash: page 9

Every effort has been made to trace copyright holders and to obtain their permission for use of copyright material. The authors and publishers would be pleased to rectify any error or omission in future editions. All the Internet addresses given in this book were correct at the time of going to press. The author and publishers regret any inconvenience caused if addresses have changed or sites have ceased to exist, but can accept no responsibility for any such changes.

Library and Archives Canada Cataloguing in Publication

Dann, Sarah, 1970-, author
    Beyoncé / Sarah Dann.

(Superstars!)
Includes index.
Issued in print and electronic formats.
ISBN 978-0-7787-0019-7 (bound).--ISBN 978-0-7787-0039-5
(pbk.).--ISBN 978-1-4271-9381-0 (pdf).--ISBN 978-1-4271-9375-9
(html)

    1. Beyoncé, 1981- --Juvenile literature. 2. Singers--United
States--Biography--Juvenile literature. 3. Rhythm and blues
musicians--United States--Biography--Juvenile literature.
I. Title. II. Series: Superstars! (St. Catharines, Ont.)

ML3930.K66D188 2013   j782.42164092   C2013-905219-4
                                            C2013-905220-8

Library of Congress Cataloging-in-Publication Data

Dann, Sarah, 1970-
  Beyonce / Sarah Dann.
       pages cm. -- (Superstars!)
  Includes index.
  ISBN 978-0-7787-0019-7 (reinforced library binding) -- ISBN
978-0-7787-0039-5 (pbk.) -- ISBN 978-1-4271-9381-0 (electronic
pdf) -- ISBN 978-1-4271-9375-9 (electronic html)
  1. Beyoncé, 1981---Juvenile literature. 2. Singers--United
States--Biography--Juvenile literature. I. Title.

ML3930.K66D36 2014
782.42164092--dc23
[B]
                                            2013030090

Crabtree Publishing Company

www.crabtreebooks.com   1-800-387-7650

Printed in Canada/102013/BF20130920

Published in Canada
Crabtree Publishing
616 Welland Ave.
St. Catharines, ON
L2M 5V6

Published in the United States
Crabtree Publishing
PMB 59051
350 Fifth Avenue, 59th Floor
New York, New York 10118

Published in the United Kingdom
Crabtree Publishing
Maritime House
Basin Road North, Hove
BN41 1WR

Published in Australia
Crabtree Publishing
3 Charles Street
Coburg North
VIC 3058

CONTENTS

Words that are defined in the glossary are in
bold type the first time they appear in the text.

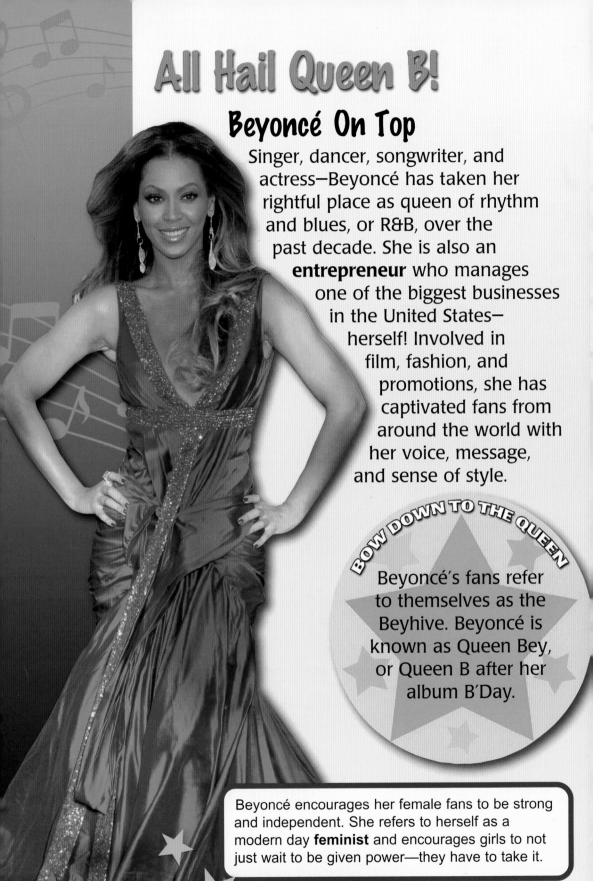

All Hail Queen B!

Beyoncé On Top

Singer, dancer, songwriter, and actress—Beyoncé has taken her rightful place as queen of rhythm and blues, or R&B, over the past decade. She is also an **entrepreneur** who manages one of the biggest businesses in the United States— herself! Involved in film, fashion, and promotions, she has captivated fans from around the world with her voice, message, and sense of style.

BOW DOWN TO THE QUEEN

Beyoncé's fans refer to themselves as the Beyhive. Beyoncé is known as Queen Bey, or Queen B after her album B'Day.

Beyoncé encourages her female fans to be strong and independent. She refers to herself as a modern day **feminist** and encourages girls to not just wait to be given power—they have to take it.

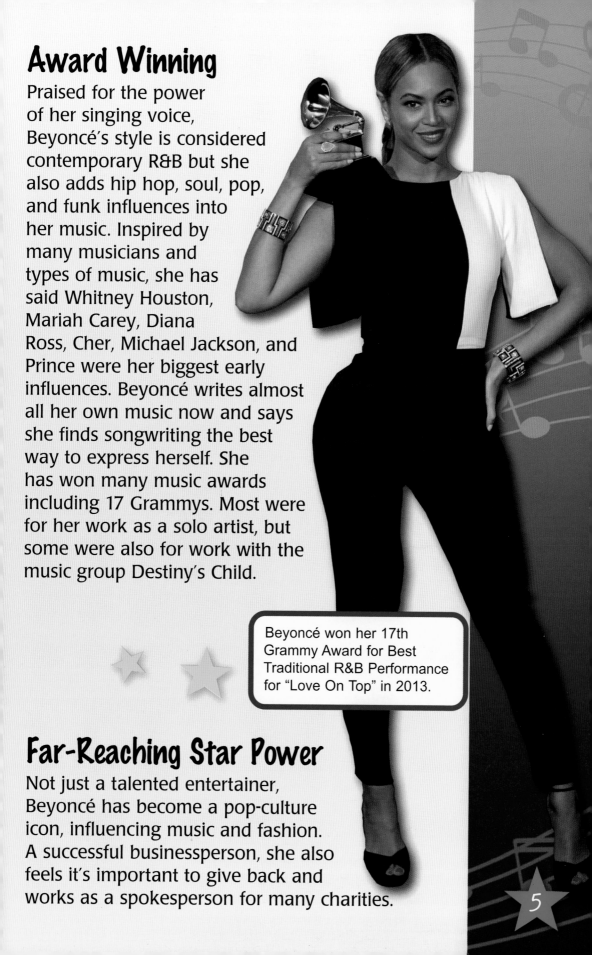

Award Winning

Praised for the power of her singing voice, Beyoncé's style is considered contemporary R&B but she also adds hip hop, soul, pop, and funk influences into her music. Inspired by many musicians and types of music, she has said Whitney Houston, Mariah Carey, Diana Ross, Cher, Michael Jackson, and Prince were her biggest early influences. Beyoncé writes almost all her own music now and says she finds songwriting the best way to express herself. She has won many music awards including 17 Grammys. Most were for her work as a solo artist, but some were also for work with the music group Destiny's Child.

Beyoncé won her 17th Grammy Award for Best Traditional R&B Performance for "Love On Top" in 2013.

Far-Reaching Star Power

Not just a talented entertainer, Beyoncé has become a pop-culture icon, influencing music and fashion. A successful businessperson, she also feels it's important to give back and works as a spokesperson for many charities.

A Family Affair

On September 4, 1981, Tina and Mathew Knowles welcomed the birth of their daughter Beyoncé Giselle Knowles. Beyoncé's first name is a **tribute** to her mother's **maiden name**, Beyincé. A sister named Solange came along five years later. The girls grew up in Houston, Texas, where their mother owned a hair salon and their father was a salesman of high-tech medical equipment. Both girls took dance classes. Beyoncé studied music and, for a time, attended private school at Houston's High School for the Performing and Visual Arts.

AMAZING RANGE

Beyoncé is a mezzo-soprano. Her singing voice ranges over three and a half **octaves**. She can hit some seriously high notes. Beyoncé's dance teacher discovered her range when she heard her humming.

Beyoncé poses with her sister Solange, and parents Tina and Mathew Knowles, at the premiere of the film *Austin Powers in Goldmember*.

Destined for Stardom

Beyoncé knew from an early age that she wanted to be a performer. When she was seven years old, she competed in a talent show and sang a song called "Imagine" by Beatles legend John Lennon. She won the contest and beat people more than twice her age! Beyoncé pursued singing by performing at school and in the church choir.

Tyme to Shine

When she was just eight years old, Beyoncé joined an all-girl rap group called Girl's Tyme. One of the members was Kelly Rowland. She and Beyoncé became good friends and, at one time, Kelly even came to live with the Knowles family.

Girl's Tyme performed in talent shows around Houston, until a music producer saw them. In 1992, he entered the group in a talent contest on a TV show called *Star Search*. The winner of the talent show would walk away with $100,000. Unfortunately, the girls did not win.

Beyoncé and Kelly Rowland remain close to this day.

She Said It

"The stability and support my parents provided when we were growing up at home has a lot to do with why Kelly and I are still around today."
—From *Soul Survivors: The Official Autobiography of Destiny's Child*

Destiny's Child Is Born

The girls were disappointed but still determined, and Beyoncé's father took over managing the group. They performed for clients in Beyoncé's mother's hair salon to perfect their song and dance routines. Eventually, the group was reduced to four members from six. Promoting the girls became a family affair for the Knowleses. Beyoncé's father eventually quit his job to be their full-time manager. Her mother Tina designed the girls' costumes.

CHANGE MY NAME

The group had many different names, including Girl's Tyme, Something Fresh, Cliché, the Dolls, and Destiny, before finding success with Destiny's Child.

A scene from *Beyoncé: Life Is But a Dream* shows Beyoncé (middle left) singing in her mom's hair salon with the original members of Destiny's Child.

PM 7:42
APR. 23 1993

Rocky Road to Success

Managing the group, however, took a toll on Beyoncé's family. When an early deal with a record label fell through, and with the family income cut in half, the stress led her parents to separate when Beyoncé was 14. Happily, by the time the group was finally signed to Columbia Records in 1997, the family had reunited.

Leaving Childhood Behind

Beyoncé left high school during ninth grade to pursue her career as a professional entertainer. By this time, the girls group had changed their name from Girl's Tyme to Destiny's Child and they were finally going to record their first album. Her dream was coming true! But Beyoncé's parents made sure she continued her education with the help of tutors. The hard-working teen finished high school by the year 2000.

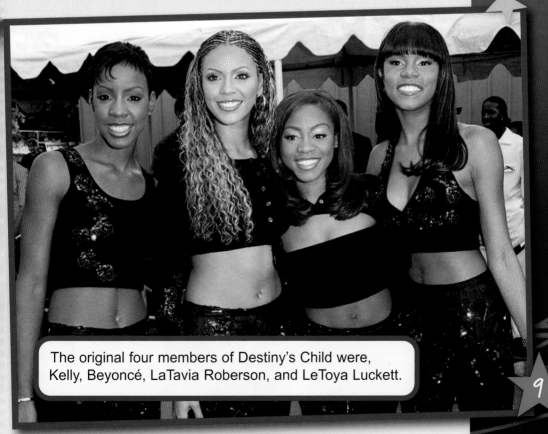

The original four members of Destiny's Child were, Kelly, Beyoncé, LaTavia Roberson, and LeToya Luckett.

No, No, No

Destiny's Child got off to a tremendous start when their first song "Killing Time" was featured in the movie *Men in Black* in 1997. The movie was a blockbuster and brought a lot of attention to the group. One year later, they released their first album *Destiny's Child* featuring their first hit song "No, No, No." The album sold one million copies in the United States and three million around the world. Destiny's Child had arrived!

Say My Name!

Striking while the iron was hot, Destiny's Child released their second album *The Writing's on the Wall* in 1999, which included the song "Say My Name." This song won a Grammy for Best R&B Song and the album sold more than eight million copies! As the group took off, Beyoncé's voice began to stand out, and she took a more active role in producing the music of Destiny's Child.

Destiny's Child won three awards at the Soul Train Lady of Soul Awards in 1998, including the best R&B Soul Album of the Year for *Destiny's Child*.

Troubled Times

Although the group was gaining a lot of attention, not everyone in Destiny's Child was happy. LeToya and LaTavia did not like the way Mathew Knowles was managing the group. The two young women wanted to find a new manager to represent the two of them while they continued their career with Destiny's Child. Instead, Mathew replaced them with two new singers—Michelle Williams and Farrah Franklin.

Yes, Yes, Yes

The new lineup of Destiny's Child went into the studio to record their third album called *Survivor*. Some felt that the album's name made reference to the survival of the band even as their members changed. In fact, Farrah Franklin was dropped after five months, leaving Beyoncé, Kelly, and Michelle as the final trio. The album debuted in spring 2001 at number one and included the hit single "Bootylicious." This song title became so popular, the word bootylicious was added to the *Oxford English Dictionary*.

SISTER ACT

Beyoncé's sister Solange often performed with Destiny's Child during times when the group's lineup was changing. She has since become a well-known singer, songwriter, and model herself.

By late 2000, Destiny's Child was a group of three, which included Michelle Williams, Kelly Rowland, and Beyoncé.

Spreading Her Wings

Beyoncé had taken on a key role in the group's last album, co-producing and co-writing all but one of the songs. Despite their success, four years of recording, touring, and promoting had caught up with them. All of the members of Destiny's Child decided to take a break to pursue individual projects. Many people thought this was the end of the group.

Add Actress

Beyoncé decided to take a turn at acting. Her first role was in 2001 in a TV musical made for MTV called *Carmen: A Hip Hopera*. Based on an opera called *Carmen*, Beyoncé played the lead character. She discovered that she liked acting and had a talent for it. She followed that up with a starring role alongside Mike Myers in the movie *Austin Powers in Goldmember* in 2002.

Beyoncé played a fun character called Foxxy Cleopatra in *Goldmember*.

She Said It

"...[Every] time I do a film I leave with more friends and more [life] experience... I didn't go to school and usually that's when you... make friends and learn about yourself and... what you like and don't like about people, so this is like my school."
—In an interview on femail.com.au about acting in films

On Her Own

In the meantime, Michelle and Kelly had each brought out solo music projects. Now it was Beyoncé's turn. At first, she found it hard to be on her own after years of working within a group. Once she got started though, Beyoncé found making an album by herself "**liberating** and **therapeutic**." She **collaborated** with other musicians and learned to express her own ideas. One of her first collaborations was with hip-hop musician Jay Z (whose real name is Shawn Carter). She sang on his song "03 Bonnie & Clyde," and they appeared together in the song's video as a couple on the run.

Beyoncé and Jay Z performed "03 Bonnie & Clyde" on MTV.

Bey and Jay

Around the time of the "03 Bonnie & Clyde" release, rumors that Beyoncé and Jay Z were dating began to spread. They had known each other professionally from Beyoncé's early days in Destiny's Child and soon became friends. In the early years of their relationship, they tried to keep their romance very private and did not talk about it publicly.

Beyoncé and Jay Z spend a date night watching the New York Knicks play basketball against the Orlando Magic on December 4, 2002.

She Said It

"We were friends first for a year and a half [before] we went on any date... And that foundation is so important in a relationship. And just to have someone that you just like, is so important. And someone that is honest."
—Interview on *Oprah's Next Chapter*

14

Dangerously in Love

In June 2003, Beyoncé released her first solo album called *Dangerously in Love*. The album contained several hits and remains her best-selling album with 11 million copies and counting sold around the world. Jay Z joined her on the album's title song. Beyoncé went on to win five Grammys for the album and toured in Europe during 2003.

MUSICAL COMEDY

Beyoncé's next film was released in 2003, the musical comedy *The Fighting Temptations*, in which she co-starred with Cuba Gooding Jr.

One Last Time

Destiny's Child decided to reunite to do a new album in 2004. *Destiny Fulfilled* turned out to be their last. During their Destiny Fulfilled... And Lovin' It Tour, they announced that the end of the tour would also be the end of Destiny's Child.

Destiny's Child performs their final concert of the Destiny Fulfilled... And Lovin' It Tour in 2005.

Fashion Forward

With the Destiny's Child chapter in her life now closed, Beyoncé looked ahead to her next project. Well known for having an excellent eye for fashion, Beyoncé joined up with her mother to create a fashion line called House of Deréon in 2005. The company name came from the surname of Beyoncé's grandmother. The line is inspired by all three generations of women in their family—grandma, mother, and Beyoncé and her sister Solange.

Tina Knowles and Beyoncé present the House of Deréon fashion show during London Fashion Week in September 2011.

B' Day

Beyoncé had a busy year in 2006. She released her second solo album, called *B'Day*. Made in just three weeks, the album was released on Beyoncé's 25th birthday. It featured the hit songs "Beautiful Liar" and "Irreplaceable." That same year, she also starred in the movie *The Pink Panther* with Steve Martin.

Dreamgirls

Beyoncé wrapped up her busy year by playing the major role of Deena Jones in the hit movie *Dreamgirls*. The movie was about an all-girl group based on The Supremes, who were a hit singing group from the 1960s. Beyoncé was nominated for a Golden Globe for her role in the film. Beyoncé released a song called "Listen" to help **promote** the film.

In *Dreamgirls*, Beyoncé played a pop star based on one of her idols—music legend Diana Ross.

She Said It

"*Diana Ross is a big inspiration to all of us. We all grew up watching everything about her—her mike placement, her grace, her style, and her class.*"
—From www.brainyquote.com

Happy Days

For most of 2007, Beyoncé was on the road on a world tour called The Beyoncé Experience to promote her album B'Day. She and Jay Z were still dating and were photographed together throughout the year. The pair seemed ideally suited. Both were very successful in their careers and were reported to be very supportive of one another. So it came as no surprise when it was revealed that the two got married in a small, very private wedding on April 4, 2008.

SIGNIFICANT NUMBER

Both Beyoncé and Jay Z have the Roman numeral IV tattooed on their ring fingers. The number 4 is significant to both of them. Her birthday is September 4, his is December 4, and their wedding day was April 4.

The Beyoncé Experience tour stopped in Seoul, South Korea, on November 9, 2007, where Beyoncé put on an energized show for fans.

Who Is Sasha Fierce?

For the rest of 2008, however, it was back to work for Beyoncé. In November, Beyoncé released her third album called *I Am...Sasha Fierce*. She created the character Sasha Fierce as an **alter ego**–the person she is on stage. She wanted her fans to know there is a difference between who she is on stage and who she is in real life. She described Sasha Fierce as being strong, sassy, and fearless.

Fierce Road Trip

I Am...Sasha Fierce received ten Grammy nominations, and the popular song "Single Ladies (Put a Ring On It)" won Song of the Year. Beyoncé hit the road for almost a year on her I Am... World Tour. She once said that "she could turn cartwheels while singing," and on stage she rarely stops moving. She has performed with the same backup dancers, called The Mamas, since 2006. Beyoncé prides herself as much on her dancing as her singing and gives 100 percent of her energy in every performance.

Performances from Beyoncé's I Am... World Tour were released on DVD.

19

More Movies

Busy Beyoncé rounded out 2008 with a role in a film called *Cadillac Records* playing Etta James—a real-life blues singer from the 1960s. Beyoncé received several award nominations for her portrayal. She later performed one of Etta James's songs at President Barack Obama's inauguration dinner in 2009. That same year, Beyoncé also had a role in a film called *Obsessed*.

Political Presence

Beyoncé has been a proud supporter of President Barack Obama. She performed the song "America, The Beautiful" at President Obama's first Presidential inauguration in 2009. She sang again at his second inauguration in 2013. This time she sang the national anthem.

Beyoncé was criticized for **lip-syncing** the national anthem at the presidential inauguration in 2013. With no time to rehearse, she felt it was the best plan.

Running the Show

Between 1993 and 2010, Beyoncé's father Mathew had worked as his daughter's manager. In 2010, Beyoncé decided to take over management of her own career. She wanted to reclaim the relationship between them as father and daughter, not business partners. Although it strained things between them, Beyoncé now oversees every aspect of her music and acting careers.

As Beyoncé and her dad were parting ways professionally, Mathew was also going through a divorce with Beyoncé's mom. The divorce was final in 2011.

Bye Bye, Sasha Fierce

Weary of recording and touring, and wanting to focus on family, Beyoncé took 2010 off "to live life, to be inspired by things again." It was June 2011 before she resurfaced with her next album. Sasha Fierce was gone. Beyoncé said she felt she knew who she was in both worlds and no longer needed Sasha's help. Just like all her previous albums, her new album—called simply *4*—debuted at number one.

She Said It

"I had to sacrifice my relationship with my dad. It was a stressful, sad, difficult time but I had to let go."
—*Beyoncé: Life Is But a Dream* documentary on HBO

Beyoncé's Baby Blue

Little did people know that when her new album *4* was released, Beyoncé was pregnant with her first child. This meant that touring to promote her new album would have to wait. Beyoncé and Jay Z became first-time parents to their daughter Blue Ivy Carter on January 7, 2012. Beyoncé says being a mother is the biggest role she has ever played, and she and Jay Z definitely want more children.

BABY BUMP

After performing her new song "Love on Top" at the VMAs, Beyoncé unbuttoned her jacket and rubbed her baby bump, announcing to the world she was pregnant!

Beyoncé's Own Words

The year 2012 was a dream come true for Beyoncé. She took the year off to be with Jay Z and their new daughter. In 2013, she returned with the release of a documentary about herself, called *Beyoncé: Life Is But a Dream*, featuring many video clips capturing parts of her private life.

Beyoncé is shown here in her home with daughter Blue Ivy during the fiming of her documentary *Beyoncé: Life Is But A Dream*.

Reunited

On February 3, 2013, Beyoncé performed during the NFL Super Bowl halftime show. Fans got a treat when her former group members, Kelly and Michelle joined her on stage to perform some of their Destiny's Child hits. The performance helped boost the sales of the Destiny's Child **compilation** album *Love Songs*, released just a week before. *Love Songs* featured songs from previous albums, as well as one new song called "Nuclear."

Mrs. Carter

Following her performance at the halftime show, Beyoncé announced to her fans that she would be setting out on another world tour called The Mrs. Carter Show World Tour. Beyoncé says the tour title is symbolic of her changing role, not only as a performer and musician, but also as a wife and mother. The tour, which began in April 2013, is scheduled to wrap up in December.

Destiny's Child reunites for a performance during Super Bowl XLVII's halftime show.

23

Busy B

Beyoncé's reach extends far beyond her music. Known for being a very smart businesswoman, *TIME* magazine described Beyoncé as one of the most influential people in the world in 2013. Her business ranges from music and movies to fashion, perfume, and **endorsement** deals.

EPIC MOVIE

Beyoncé recently created the voice for Queen Tara in the animated movie *Epic*, released in May 2013. Her song "Rise Up" is part of the soundtrack for the movie.

Perfumes

Beyoncé has currently developed six women's perfumes that are part of the fragance lines Heat and Pulse. Her Heat fragrances have been named the number-one-selling celebrity fragrances in the world. Her latest perfume Beyoncé Heat The Mrs. Carter Show World Tour is a limited-edition fragrance named for her world tour.

Beyoncé's perfume Heat was her first fragrance released in Februrary 2010.

Cover Girl

Beyoncé spends so much time dancing and performing that she is in great shape. She has appeared on numerous magazine covers such as *Vogue, Glamour*, and *Vanity Fair*. She was also the second African-American woman to appear on the cover of *Sports Illustrated's* Swimsuit Issue. In 2013, men's magazine *GQ* placed her on their 100 Sexiest Women of the 21st Century list.

In 2012, Beyoncé was named the World's Most Beautiful Woman by *People* magazine.

Endorsements

Beyoncé's popularity has also landed her a number of endorsement deals. She has worked with L'Oréal since she was 18 years old, promoting its beauty products. She also has done endorsement deals for H&M, American Express, Wal-Mart, McDonald's, and Nintendo.

Helping Girls

Beyoncé supports several charities aimed specifically at helping girls. Chime for Change is an international organization that was founded

by fashion giant Gucci. They work to promote education, health, and justice for every girl and every woman—everywhere. Beyoncé also works with Girl Up—a group that organizes clubs and events for American girls that in turn help girls around the world have better lives. Haiti Adolescent Girls Network, Girls Inc. of Houston, and Elevate of New York, are other organizations Beyoncé supports.

On June 1, 2013, Chime for Change held a live concert called Sound of Change Live. Beyoncé was just one of the performers helping out this worthy cause.

She Said It

"Reaching out and touching lives is incredibly empowering. That's why I want my fans to experience the joy of making a difference by helping someone else."
—In an article on www.seventeen.com

Helping Disaster Relief

In 2005, after Hurricane Katrina devastated New Orleans, Beyoncé and Kelly Rowland joined together to found the Survivor Foundation. The foundation provided temporary housing for hurricane survivors who had ended up in the Houston area. The Survivor Foundation has raised millions of dollars to help families get back on their feet after disasters.

After an earthquake caused widespread destruction in Haiti in 2010, Beyoncé lent her support to the country's recovery. She became the official face of a "Fashion for Haiti" T-shirt which raised $1 million for the relief effort.

Beyoncé also performed at the Hope for Haiti Now **telethon** to help raise money for Haiti's earthquake victims.

Around the World

Beyoncé was also the ambassador for the 2012 World **Humanitarian** Day—a day dedicated to people working for humanitarian causes and honoring people who have lost their lives doing so. Beyoncé helped the event make social media history when more than one billion messages were shared at one time about the event.

Continuing Success

Forbes magazine listed Beyoncé and husband Jay Z at the top of the list for highest-earning Hollywood couples in 2013. Hard work and business smarts have put Beyoncé on top. What's next? While jetting around the world on The Mrs. Carter Show World Tour, Beyoncé has also been working on her fifth album. She has been quoted as saying she would like to win an Oscar one day. But the busy mother-of-one also says she would like to add to her family in the near future.

"I definitely want to have another child. But it's also important for me to do what I love. I love to make music. I wanted to see, after I had my daughter, if I was still as passionate about performing. Maybe after this next tour I'll have another."
—In an interview on Oprah's Next Chapter

Beyoncé dazzles her fans in New York City while performing on one of her many stops of The Mrs. Carter Show World Tour.

Timeline

1981: Beyoncé Giselle Knowles is born in Houston, Texas, on September 21

1990: Joins a girl band called Girl's Tyme

1992: Girl's Tyme compete on *Star Search*, but don't win

1997: Girl band now called Destiny's Child signs with Columbia Records

1998: Destiny's Child releases their first album *Destiny's Child*

1999: Destiny's Child releases their second album *The Writing on the Wall*

2001: Destiny's Child releases their third album entitled *Survivor*

2002: Plays Foxxy Cleopatra in *Austin Powers in Goldmember*

2003: Releases first solo album *Dangerously in Love*

2003: Plays Lilly in *The Fighting Temptations*

2004: Destiny's Child releases their fourth album *Destiny Fulfilled*

2006: Releases her second album *B'Day*

2006: Plays Deena Jones in *Dreamgirls*

2006: Plays Xania in *The Pink Panther*

2008: Marries Jay Z (Shawn Carter) on April 4

2008: Plays Etta James in *Cadillac Records*

2008: Releases her third solo album *I Am... Sasha Fierce*

2009: Performs at Presidential Inauguration

2009: Plays Sharon Charles in *Obsessed*

2011: Releases her fourth album *4*

2012: Gives birth to Blue Ivy on January 7

2013: Performs at Presidential Inauguration

2013: Destiny's Child releases album *Love Songs*

2013: Performs during the halftime show of Super Bowl XLVII

2013: Provides the voice of Queen Tara in *Epic*

2013: Releases documentary *Beyoncé: Life Is But a Dream*

Glossary

alter-ego Another aspect of your self or personality

collaborated Worked with another person on a project

compilation Something that contains material from various sources or places

endorsement Approval or supporting something

entrepreneur Someone who owns, runs, or manages a business

feminist Someone who believes men and women should be treated equally

humanitarian Relating to people who are concerned for the well-being of others and working to help others in need

liberating Releasing, letting loose, or setting free

lip-syncing When the lips move to a recorded song

maiden name A woman's last name before she gets married

octaves Units of seven notes each used in music that range from high to low

promote To share information about a product to help sell it

therapeutic Benefiting someone's mental state, such as to calm or relax them

tribute Something done to show respect or give thanks

Find Out More

Books

Landau, Elaine. *Beyoncé: R & B Superstar*. Lerner
    Publishing, 2013.

Tieck, Sarah. *Famous Actress/Singer: Infinite Romance*.
    ABDO Publishing, 2009.

Websites

Beyoncé
    www.Beyoncé.com
The official Beyoncé website includes music, lyrics,
news, photos, and access to the Beyhive blog.

Fan Site
    www.theBeyoncénetwork.com
One of the most active fan sites for Beyoncé

Beyoncé
    www.girlup.org
One of the most active charities Beyoncé supports

Index

About the Author

Sarah Dann publishes her own magazine and writes a variety of articles for various publications. She attended university to perfect her writing skills by studying English and Journalism. Sarah has written several titles and found the Superstars! series to be particularly inspiring with their message of working hard to get amazing results.